AF893925

SCALES MADE SIMPLE

A LOGICAL APPROACH TO LEARNING SCALES

Alfred

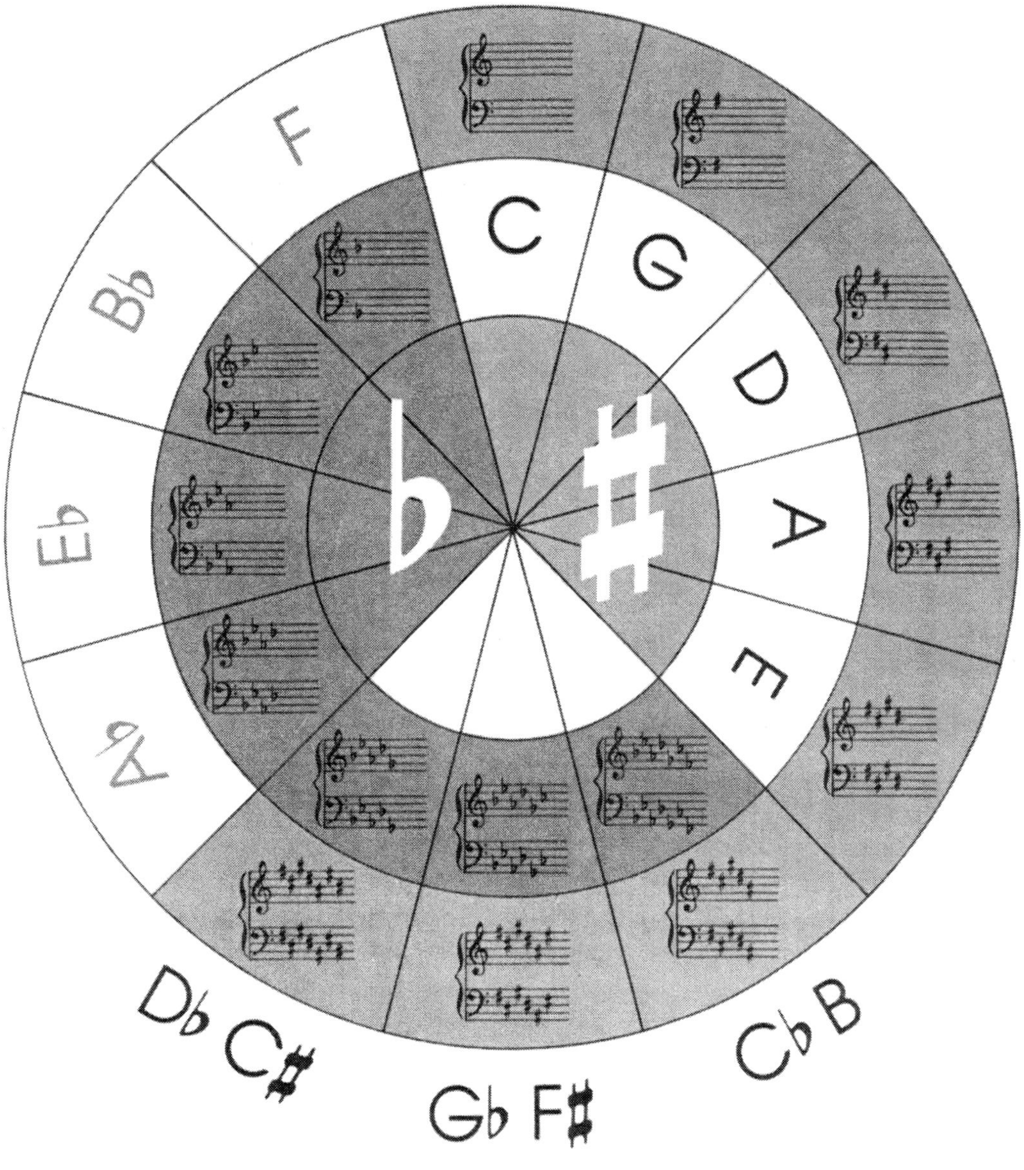

CONTENTS

FOREWORD

This method was designed to organize the learning of key signatures and scale fingerings into orderly, logical, and easily remembered patterns. Its simple principles will enable the student to find all key signatures without tedious memorization and to finger scales with only a few basic rules.

Traditional fingering is taught, but for an entire group of scales, so that one rule applies to as many as twelve. (For example: all major scales for the right hand require only two fingerings—with no exceptions. All major scales for the left hand require only three fingerings—with no exceptions. Most minor scales are fingered like their parallel major scales, making it unnecessary to relearn their fingerings.) The scales are not printed in notation, which averts the student's memorizing each one separately.

SCALES MADE SIMPLE is applicable to students on all levels of proficiency. A first-year student is taught to understand and to play all the major scales in tetrachords. An intermediate student is taught key signatures and traditional fingerings in systematic and organized groupings. An advanced student or teacher may use SCALES MADE SIMPLE as a concise reference.

CIRCLE OF FIFTHS
MAJOR SCALES

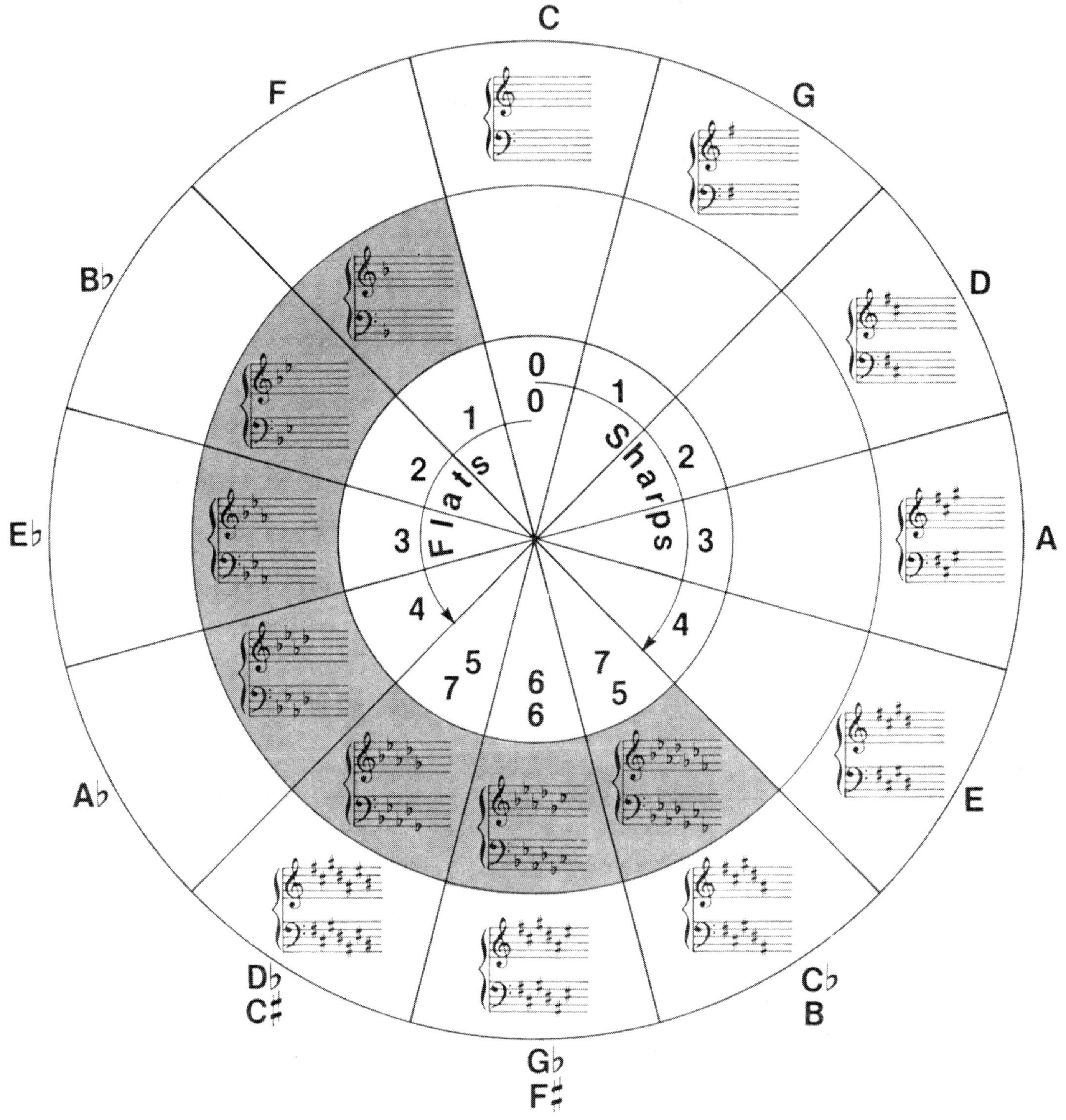

CIRCLE OF FIFTHS

Knowing key signatures and scales can be as easy as telling time. The circle of fifths resembles a clock.

MAJOR SCALES USING SHARPS

The clock shows:

- 12 as the starting point.
- five-minute intervals as the long hand progresses clockwise.
- one hour added as the short hand progresses clockwise.
- the number of the hour.

The circle of fifths shows:

- C major as the starting point.
- intervals of a fifth.
- one sharp added to the key signature for each fifth progressing clockwise.
- the number of sharps in the key signature.

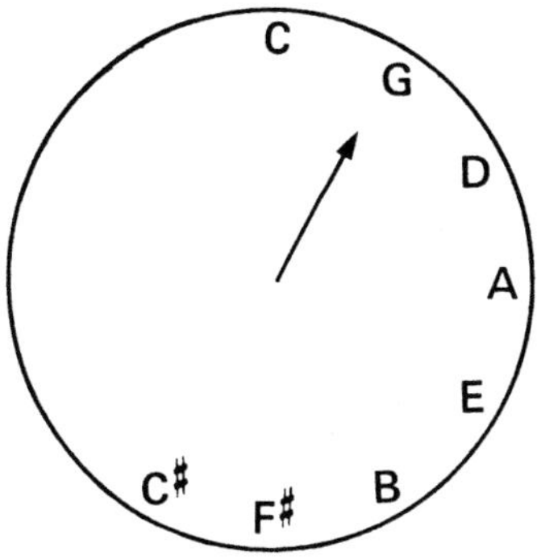

THINGS TO DO:

- On the keyboard play ascending fifths beginning with C and ending with C♯. Use R.H. fingers 1 and 5. The top note of each fifth is the tonic in the new scale, and one sharp is added to the key signature.
- As you play say the name of the key and the number of sharps in the signature. (C – 0; G – 1; D – 2; etc.)

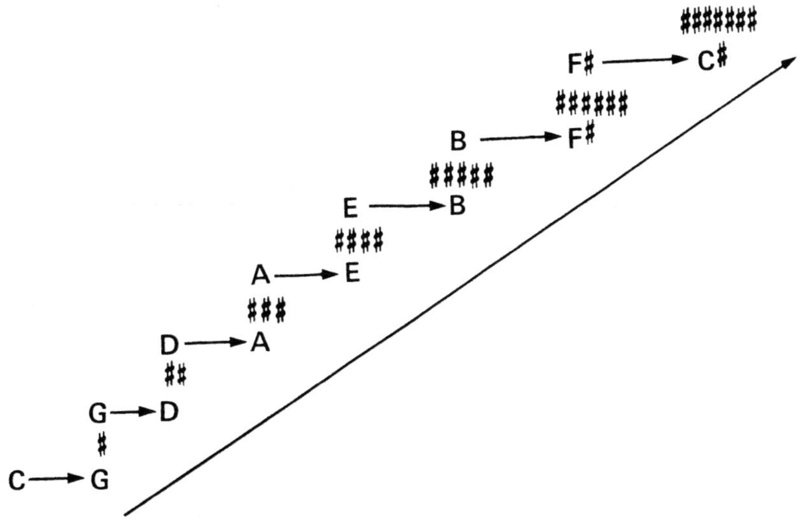

> ***REMEMBER:***
>
> - C major has 0 sharps.
> - Ascend in fifths from C, and add one sharp to the key signature.

MAJOR SCALES USING FLATS

Flat scales also use the first seven numbers on the clock. However, they progress counterclockwise. Again using C as the starting point one flat is added to the key signature for each fifth progressing counterclockwise around the circle. (Three flats—E♭ major—three o'clock counterclockwise.)

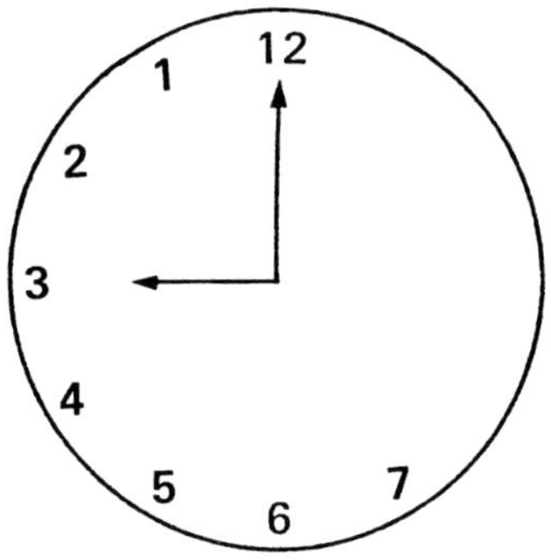

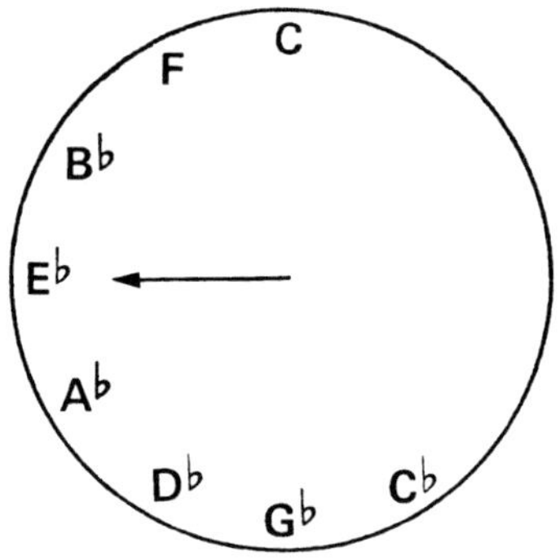

THINGS TO DO:

- On the keyboard play descending fifths beginning with C and ending with C♭. Use L.H. fingers 1 and 5. The bottom note of each fifth is the tonic in the new scale, and one flat is added to the key signature.
- As you play say the name of the key and the number of flats in the signature. (C – 0; F – 1; B♭ – 2; E♭ – 3; etc.)

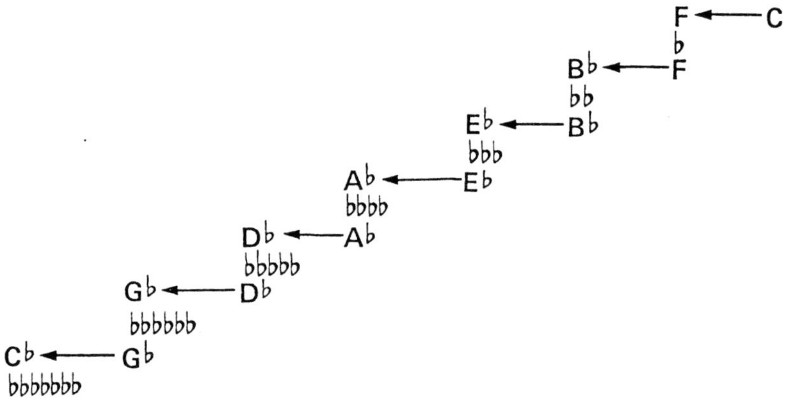

> ***REMEMBER:***
> - C major has 0 flats.
> - Descend in fifths from C, and add one flat to the key signature.

ENHARMONIC SCALES

The final three sharp scales and the final three flat scales overlap. C♯/D♭, F♯/G♭, and B/C♭ are called enharmonic scales. The keys on the keyboard, the sounds, and the fingering are the same, but the written appearance is different.

C♯/D♭ Major Scales

C♯	D♯	E♯	F♯	G♯	A♯	B♯	C♯
D♭	E♭	F	G♭	A♭	B♭	C	D♭

F♯/G♭ Major Scales

F♯	G♯	A♯	B	C♯	D♯	E♯	F♯
G♭	A♭	B♭	C♭	D♭	E♭	F	G♭

B/C♭ Major Scales

B	C♯	D♯	E	F♯	G♯	A♯	B
C♭	D♭	E♭	F♭	G♭	A♭	B♭	C♭

FINDING KEY SIGNATURES

SHARPS

Sharps are added into the key signature beginning with F♯ on the keyboard and ascending in fifths.

THINGS TO DO:

- On the keyboard play ascending fifths beginning with F♯ and ending with B♯ . Use R.H. fingers 1 and 5.
- Say the names of the sharps as you play.

F♯ → C♯ → G♯ → D♯ → A♯ → E♯ → B♯

> ***REMEMBER:***
> - F♯ is the first sharp.
> - Ascend in fifths from F♯ to add each new sharp to the signature.

FLATS

Flats are added into the key signature beginning with B♭ on the keyboard and descending in fifths.

THINGS TO DO:

- On the keyboard play descending fifths beginning with B♭ and ending with F♭ . Use L.H. fingers 1 and 5.
- Say the names of the flats as you play.

B♭ → E♭ → A♭ → D♭ → G♭ → C♭ → F♭

> ***REMEMBER:***
> - B♭ is the beginning flat.
> - Descend in fifths from B♭ to add each new flat to the signature.

BUILDING MAJOR SCALES IN TETRACHORDS

The major scale is composed of two tetrachords connected by a whole step. Each tetrachord consists of four notes arranged in this order:

whole step – whole step – half step

The pattern for the major scale is:

First tetrachord	Connecting whole step	Second tetrachord
W W H	W	W W H

The fingering used for learning major scales in tetrachords is:

Left Hand: 5 4 3 2   Right Hand: 2 3 4 5
The thumb is folded gently under the hand.

```
                            2 3 4 5
( L.H.  C D E F     R.H.    G A B C )
        5 4 3 2
```

THINGS TO DO:

- Play the sharp major scales in order around the circle of fifths. Allow the top tetrachord of one scale to become the bottom tetrachord of the new scale.
- Say the pattern as you play each scale.

```
C  D  E  F      2  3  4  5
5  4  3  2      G  A  B  C

G  A  B  C      2  3  4  5
5  4  3  2      D  E  F# G

D  E  F# G      2  3  4  5
5  4  3  2      A  B  C# D

A  B  C# D      2  3  4  5
5  4  3  2      E  F# G# A

E  F# G# A      2  3  4  5
5  4  3  2      B  C# D# E

B  C# D# E      2  3  4  5
5  4  3  2      F# G# A# B

F# G# A# B      2  3  4  5
5  4  3  2      C# D# E# F#

C# D# E# F#     2  3  4  5
5  4  3  2      G# A# B# C#
```

THINGS TO DO:

- Play the flat major scales in order around the circle of fifths. Allow the bottom tetrachord of one scale to become the top tetrachord of the new scale.
- Say the pattern as you play.

2 3 4 5
C D E F — G A B C
5 4 3 2

2 3 4 5
F G A B♭ — C D E F
5 4 3 2

2 3 4 5
B♭ C D E♭ — F G A B♭
5 4 3 2

2 3 4 5
E♭ F G A♭ — B♭ C D E♭
5 4 3 2

2 3 4 5
A♭ B♭ C D♭ — E♭ F G A♭
5 4 3 2

2 3 4 5
D♭ E♭ F G♭ — A♭ B♭ C D♭
5 4 3 2

2 3 4 5
G♭ A♭ B♭ C♭ — D♭ E♭ F G♭
5 4 3 2

2 3 4 5
C♭ D♭ E♭ F♭ — G♭ A♭ B♭ C♭
5 4 3 2

REMEMBER:

Major scale pattern:
whole step — whole step — half step .... whole step .... whole step — whole step — half step

LEARNING TO PLAY MAJOR SCALES

THINGS TO DO ON PAGES 11 THROUGH 16:

LEARN THOROUGHLY ALL MAJOR SCALES, *HANDS SEPARATELY,* ONE OCTAVE.

A. **Learn all scales in one fingering group together, L.H. first, then R.H.**
   1. Practice ~~them~~ ascending in half notes. Rest two counts at the top, and descend in half notes.
   2. Ascend in quarter notes, rest two counts, and descend in quarters.
   3. Ascend in eighth notes, rest two counts, and descend in eighths.

B. **Increase the number of octaves the scales are played.**
   1. Practice all scales in one fingering group two octaves in half notes.
   2. Practice them one octave in quarter notes.
   3. Practice them two octaves in eighth notes.
   4. Practice them three octaves in triplet eighth notes.
   5. Practice them four octaves in sixteenth notes.

C. **Vary the articulation, dynamics, and direction.**
   1. Practice all scales in one fingering group legato. Play the top note of the scale quieter and lift the wrist as if ending a phrase. Descend and play the bottom note quieter using a wrist lift to end the scale.
   2. Practice all scales in one group staccato.
   3. Practice them portato.
   4. Begin the scale pianissimo and crescendo to forte at the top. Diminuendo as the scale descends, returning to piano.
   5. Begin the scale forte and diminuendo to pianissimo at the top. Crescendo as the scale descends, returning to forte.
   6. Select a dynamic level and maintain it evenly ascending. Select a different level and control it evenly descending.
   7. Make up your own dynamics and combine them with any of the above articulations. Be sure to make your plan before you play. Listen while you play to be sure that the plan was achieved in sound.
   8. Begin the scale at its top key and descend first. Finish by ascending to the starting key. Plan and play with dynamics and articulation.

Be sure to keep the same, steady pulse for all the different note values. The metronome may be used. Proceed to quicker note values *only* when the slower ones are smooth, even, and easy to play.

MAJOR SCALES – LEFT HAND

Learn only one rule to play all six of these scales.

THE FOURTH FINGER PLAYS THE SECOND NOTE OF THE SCALE. THIS NOTE IS JUST ABOVE THE TONIC.

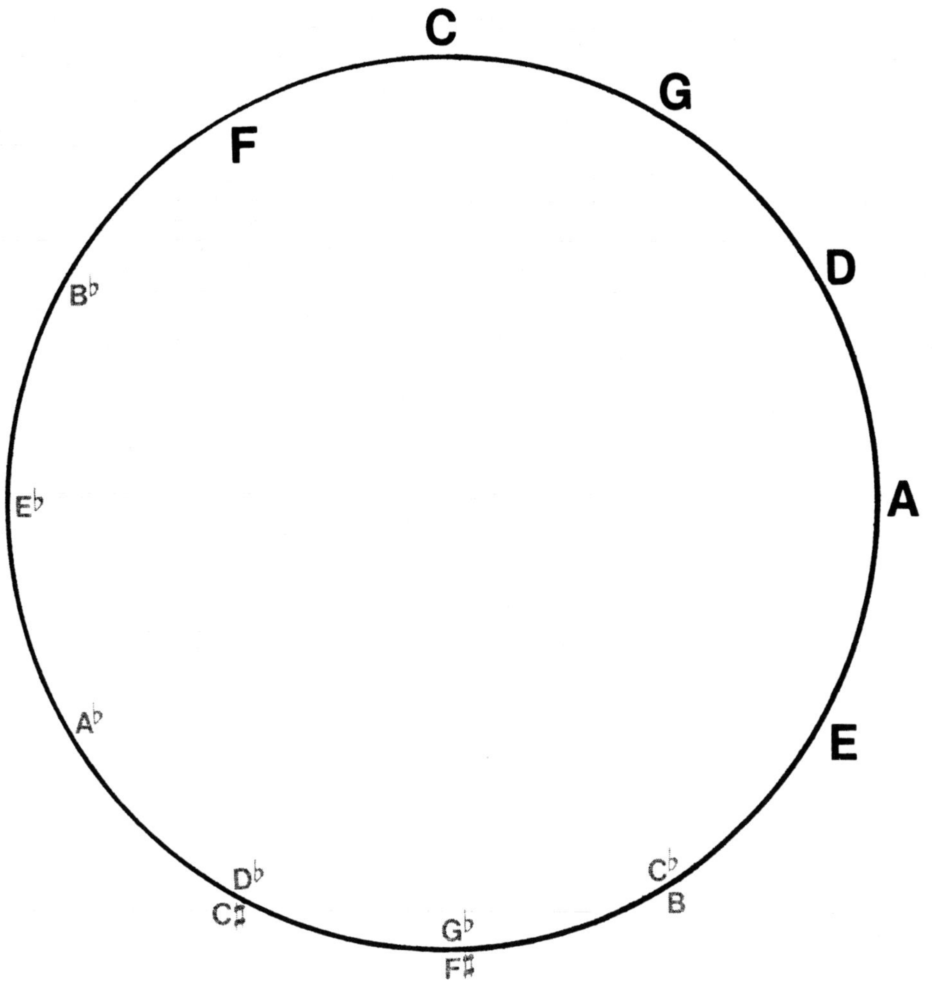

REMEMBER:
4th on 2nd note

MAJOR SCALES — LEFT HAND

Learn the *Rule of 3 Black Keys* to play these six scales.

RULE OF 3 BLACK KEYS:

THE FOURTH FINGER OF THE LEFT HAND PLAYS THE LOWEST KEY OF THE THREE BLACK KEY GROUP.

To discover the beginning finger, place the fourth finger on G♭/F♯ and descend to the tonic. (Example: C♭/B Major – play 4 on G♭/F♯, cross 1 under on F♭/E, 2 on E♭/D♯, 3 on D♭/C♯, 4 on C♭/B. 4 is the beginning finger.)

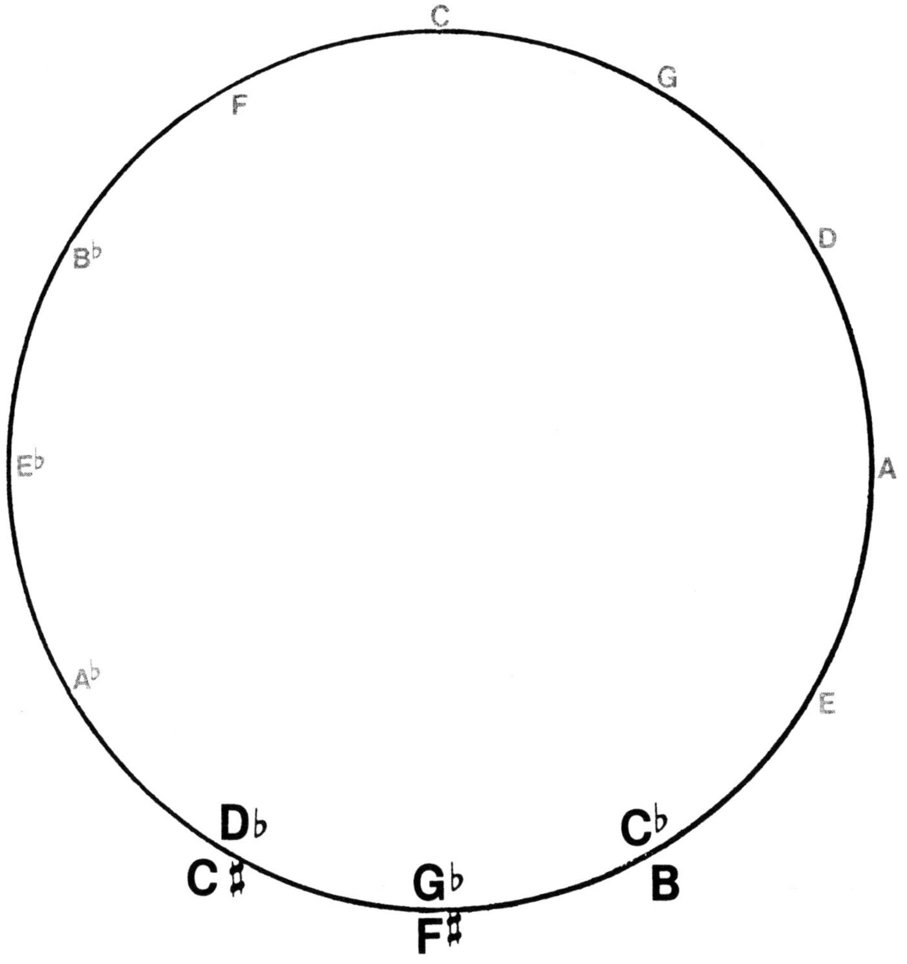

REMEMBER:

Rule of 3 Black Keys

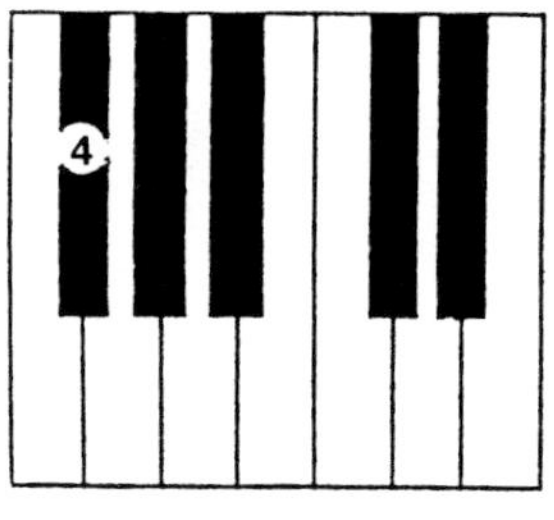

MAJOR SCALES — LEFT HAND

Learn only one rule to play these three scales.

THE FOURTH FINGER PLAYS THE FOURTH NOTE OF THE SCALE. THIS NOTE IS ALWAYS THE NEWEST FLAT IN THE KEY SIGNATURE.

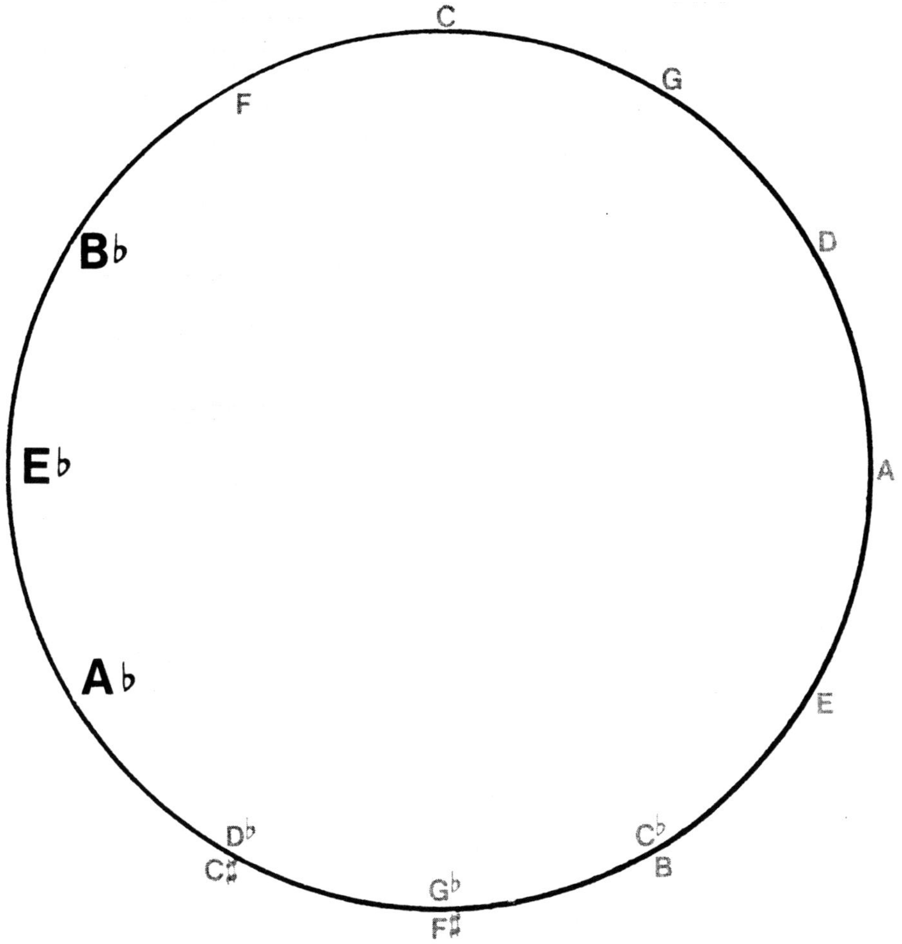

REMEMBER:
4th on 4th note

MAJOR SCALES — RIGHT HAND

Learn one rule for these five scales.

THE FOURTH FINGER PLAYS THE SEVENTH NOTE OF THE SCALE. THIS NOTE IS JUST BELOW THE TONIC.

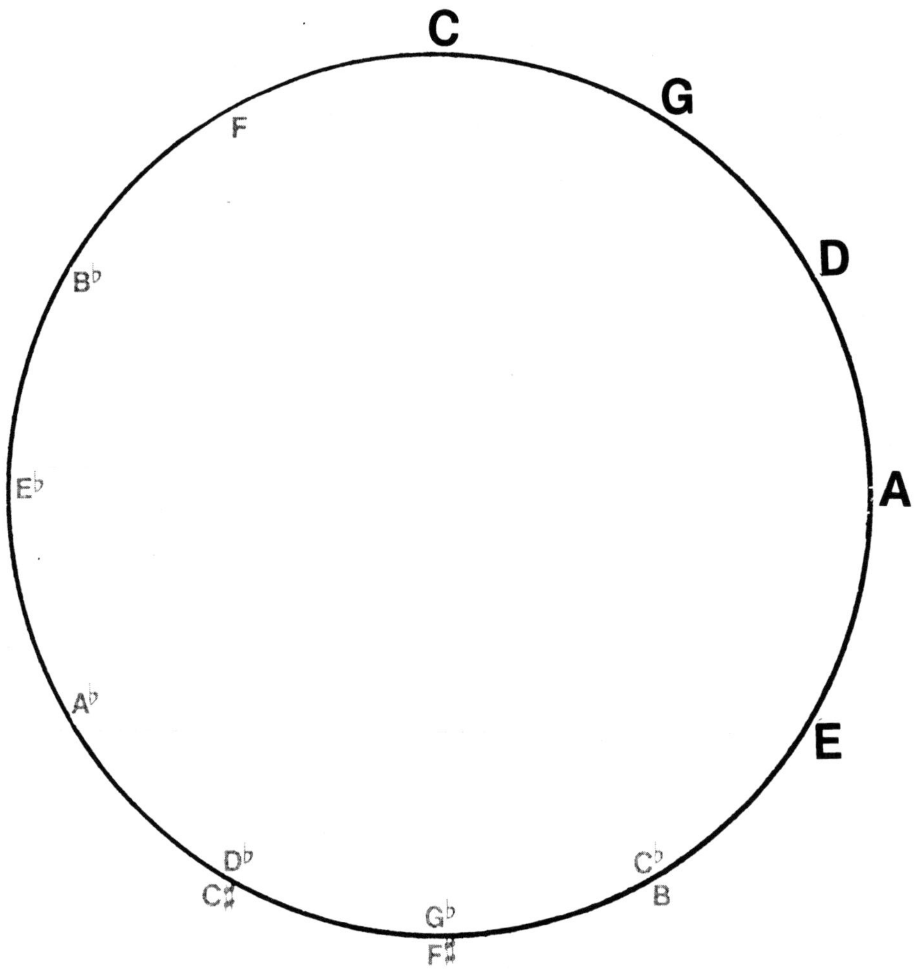

> ***REMEMBER:***
> 4th on the 7th note

MAJOR SCALES — RIGHT HAND

Learn only one rule for every major scale containing flats.

THE FOURTH FINGER OF THE RIGHT HAND PLAYS B♭ (A♯ ENHARMONICALLY) IN EVERY MAJOR SCALE CONTAINING FLATS.

To discover the beginning finger, place the fourth finger on B♭ and descend to the tonic. (Example: E♭ Major – play 4 on B♭ , 3 on A♭ , 2 on G, 1 on F, cross over 3 on E♭. 3 is the beginning finger.)

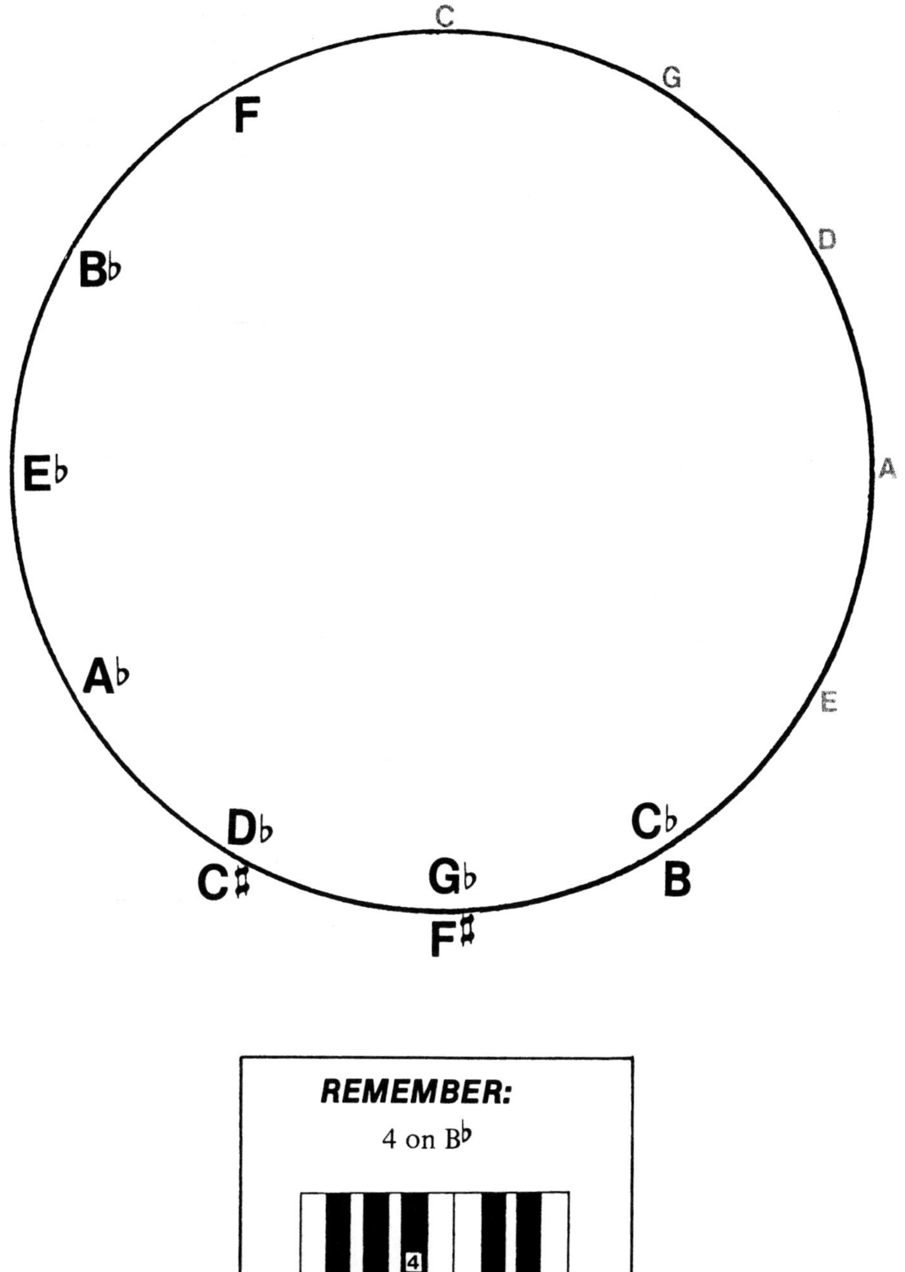

REMEMBER:

4 on B♭

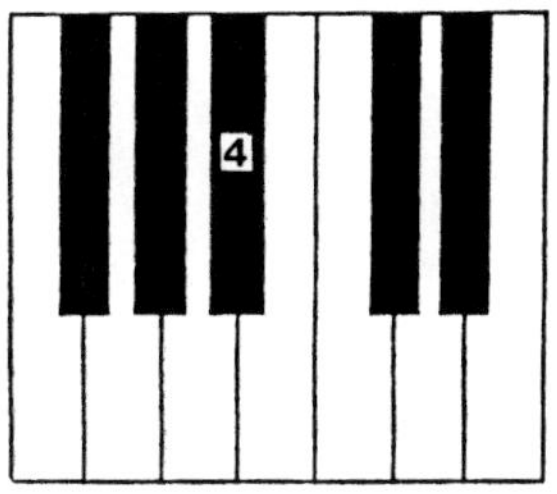

CIRCLE OF 5THS
MAJOR SCALE FINGERING — SUMMARY

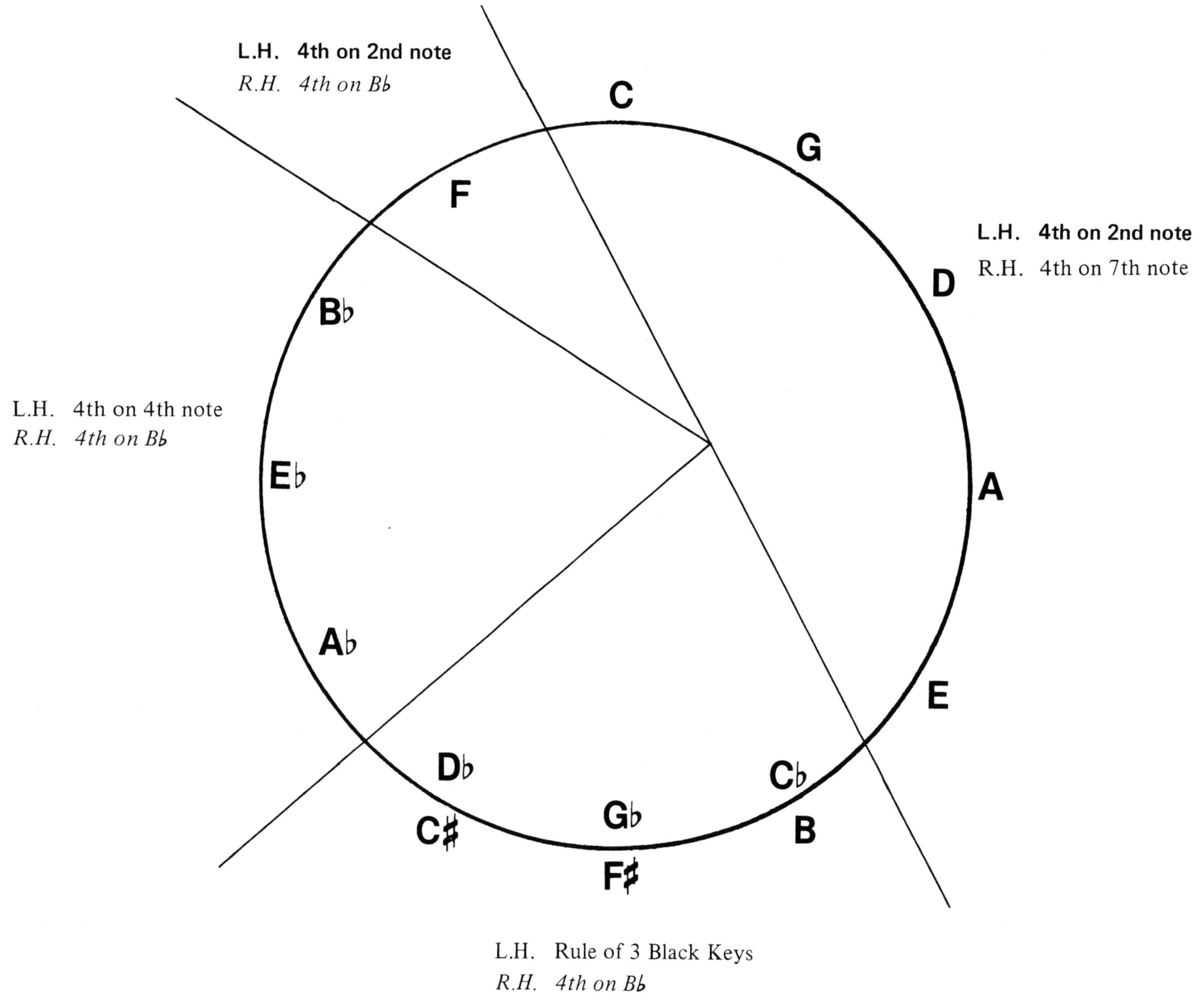

LEARNING TO PLAY MAJOR SCALES

THINGS TO DO ON PAGES 18 AND 19:

I. LEARN ALL THE MAJOR SCALES, HANDS TOGETHER, ONE OCTAVE. LEARN ALL SCALES IN ONE FINGERING GROUP TOGETHER. PRACTICE THEM IN HALF NOTES, QUARTER NOTES, AND EIGHTH NOTES.

Always keep the pulse steady. Learn the scales thoroughly one octave in half notes before proceeding to quicker note values and two octaves.

A. Group 1 contains C, G, D, A, and E.

B. Group 2 contains F, B/C♭, F♯/G♭, and C♯/D♭.

C. Group 3 contains B♭, E♭, and A♭. These three scales should be learned one at a time.

II. INCREASE THE NUMBER OF OCTAVES.

A. Practice all scales in one group two octaves in half notes.

B. Practice them one octave in quarter notes.

C. Practice them two octaves in eighth notes.

D. Practice them three octaves in triplet eighth notes.

E. Practice them four octaves in sixteenth notes.

III. VARY THE DIRECTION, THE INTERVALS BETWEEN THE HANDS, THE ARTICULATION, THE DYNAMICS, AND THE RHYTHM. PRACTICE ALL SCALES IN ONE FINGERING GROUP TOGETHER.

A. Play them in contrary motion, beginning on the same key near the center of the piano, playing in opposite directions one octave out and back. Increase to two octaves.

B. Begin the scale at its top key and descend in parallel motion first. Complete by ascending to the starting key.

C. In parallel motion, ascend two octaves. Continue, without breaking the pulse, two octaves in contrary motion out and back. Then descend two octaves to the point of origin never stopping the pulse.

D. Using the original fingering, practice the scales in parallel motion with the hands separated at the interval of a tenth (Example: C Major–L.H. begins on C using finger 5. R.H. begins on E, a tenth higher, using finger 3); the interval of a third (Example: C Major–L.H. begins on C using finger 5. R.H. begins on E, a third higher, using finger 3); the interval of a sixth (Example: C Major–L.H. begins on E using finger 3. R.H. begins on C, a sixth higher, using finger 1.)

E. Practice the scales in parallel motion legato, making the top note and the bottom note quieter. Practice them staccato. Practice them portato.

F. Combine different articulations. (Example: L.H. legato and R.H. staccato.)

G. Make your own plan for dynamics using all degrees of piano, forte, crescendo, and diminuendo.

H. Let the L.H. play ascending quarter notes one octave while the R.H. plays eighths ascending two octaves; triplet eighths ascending three octaves; sixteenth notes ascending four octaves.

I. Let the R.H. play descending quarter notes one octave while the L.H. plays eighths descending two octaves; triplet eighths descending three octaves; sixteenth notes ascending four octaves.

J. Let the L.H. ascend in duple eighths while the R.H. ascends in triplet eighths. Descend.

K. Let the R.H. descend in duple eighths while the L.H. descends in triplet eighths. Ascend.

L. Make your own combinations of the above varied directions, interval separations, articulations, dynamics, and rhythms.

MAJOR SCALES
HANDS TOGETHER — PARALLEL MOTION

When playing scales hands together it is helpful to notice that:

(1) Scales always use alternating groups of three and four fingers.
(1 2 3) (1 2 3 4) or (1 2 3 4) (1 2 3)

(2) In most scales certain same fingers will always play together.

Notice in the following group of scales:

(1) Third fingers always play together.

(2) Fourth fingers surround the tonic. (L.H. 4 is above the tonic. R.H. 4 is below the tonic.)

	1	2	3	1	2	3	4	5(1)
C	C	D	E	F	G	A	B	C
	5(1)	4	3	2	1	3	2	1

	1	2	3	1	2	3	4	5(1)
G	G	A	B	C	D	E	F♯	G
	5(1)	4	3	2	1	3	2	1

	1	2	3	1	2	3	4	5(1)
D	D	E	F♯	G	A	B	C♯	D
	5(1)	4	3	2	1	3	2	1

	1	2	3	1	2	3	4	5(1)
A	A	B	C♯	D	E	F♯	G♯	A
	5(1)	4	3	2	1	3	2	1

	1	2	3	1	2	3	4	5(1)
E	E	F♯	G♯	A	B	C♯	D♯	E
	5(1)	4	3	2	1	3	2	1

Notice in the following group of scales:
(1) Thumbs always play together.

F	1	2	3	4	1	2	3	4(1)
	F	G	A	B♭	C	D	E	F
	5(1)	4	3	2	1	3	2	1

	1	2	3	1	2	3	4	5(1)
B	B	C♯	D♯	E	F♯	G♯	A♯	B
C♭	C♭	D♭	E♭	F♭	G♭	A♭	B♭	C♭
	4(1)	3	2	1	4	3	2	1

	2	3	4	1	2	3	1	2
F♯	F♯	G♯	A♯	B	C♯	D♯	E♯	F♯
G♭	G♭	A♭	B♭	C♭	D♭	E♭	F	G♭
	4	3	2	1	3	2	1	4

	2	3	1	2	3	4	1	2
C♯	C♯	D♯	E♯	F♯	G♯	A♯	B♯	C♯
D♭	D♭	E♭	F	G♭	A♭	B♭	C	D♭
	3	2	1	4	3	2	1	3

Notice in this scale:
(1) Third and fourth fingers play together on the black keys.
(2) Second fingers are together on G.

B♭	4	1	2	3	1	2	3	4
	B♭	C	D	E♭	F	G	A	B♭
	3	2	1	4	3	2	1	3

Notice in this scale:
(1) Third fingers play together on E♭.
(2) Third and fourth fingers play together on the remaining black keys.

E♭	3	1	2	3	4	1	2	3
	E♭	F	G	A♭	B♭	C	D	E♭
	3	2	1	4	3	2	1	3

Notice in this scale:
(1) Third fingers always play together.

A♭	3	4	1	2	3	1	2	3
	A♭	B♭	C	D♭	E♭	F	G	A♭
	3	2	1	4	3	2	1	3

CIRCLE OF FIFTHS
MINOR SCALES

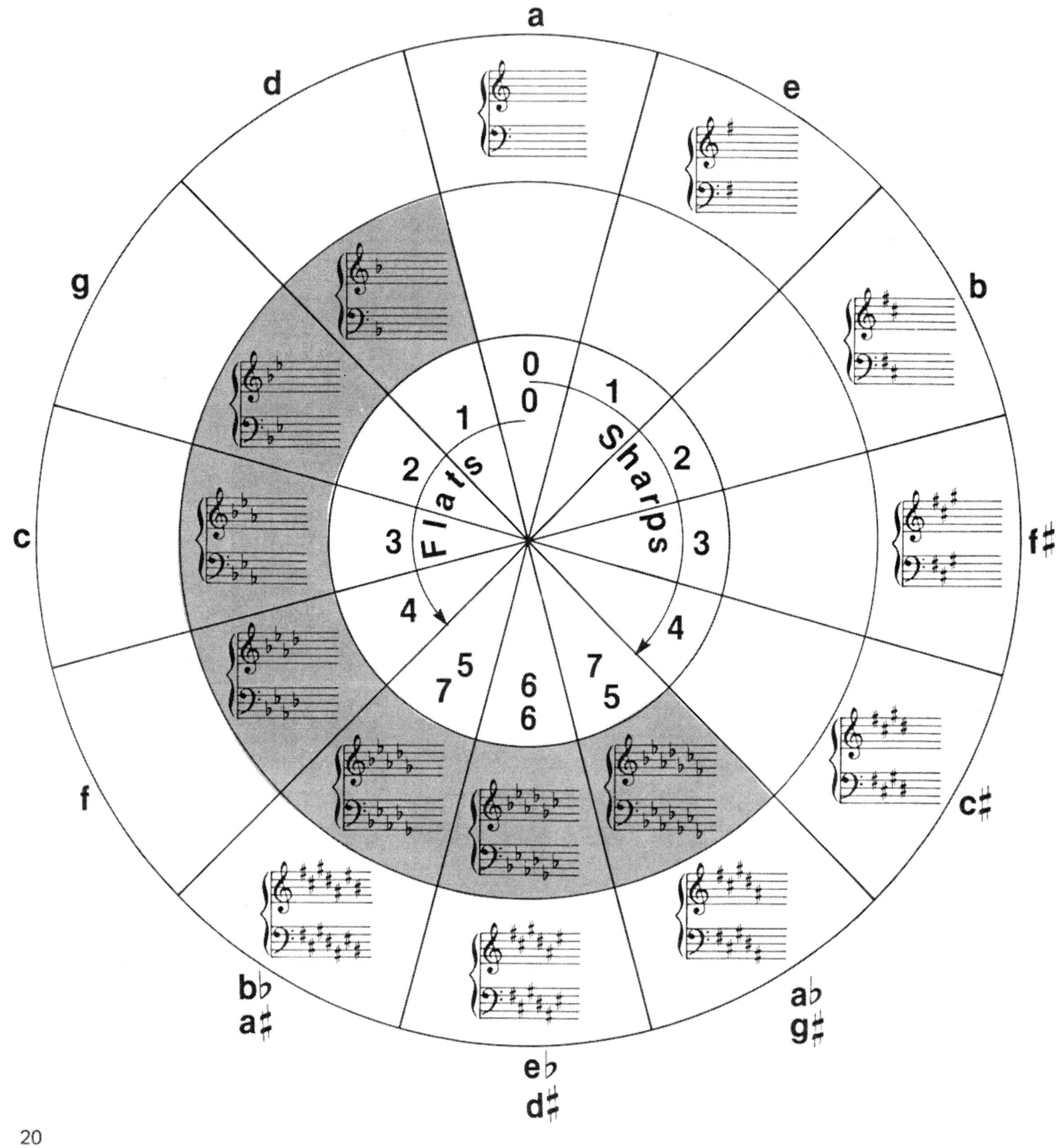

MINOR SCALES

Minor scales are related to major scales in either of two ways:

(1) Parallel minor scales have the same tonic note as the major. (C major—C minor)

(2) Relative minor scales are built on the sixth note of the major scale and have the same key signature as the major scale. (C major—A minor)

RELATIVE MAJOR AND MINOR SCALES

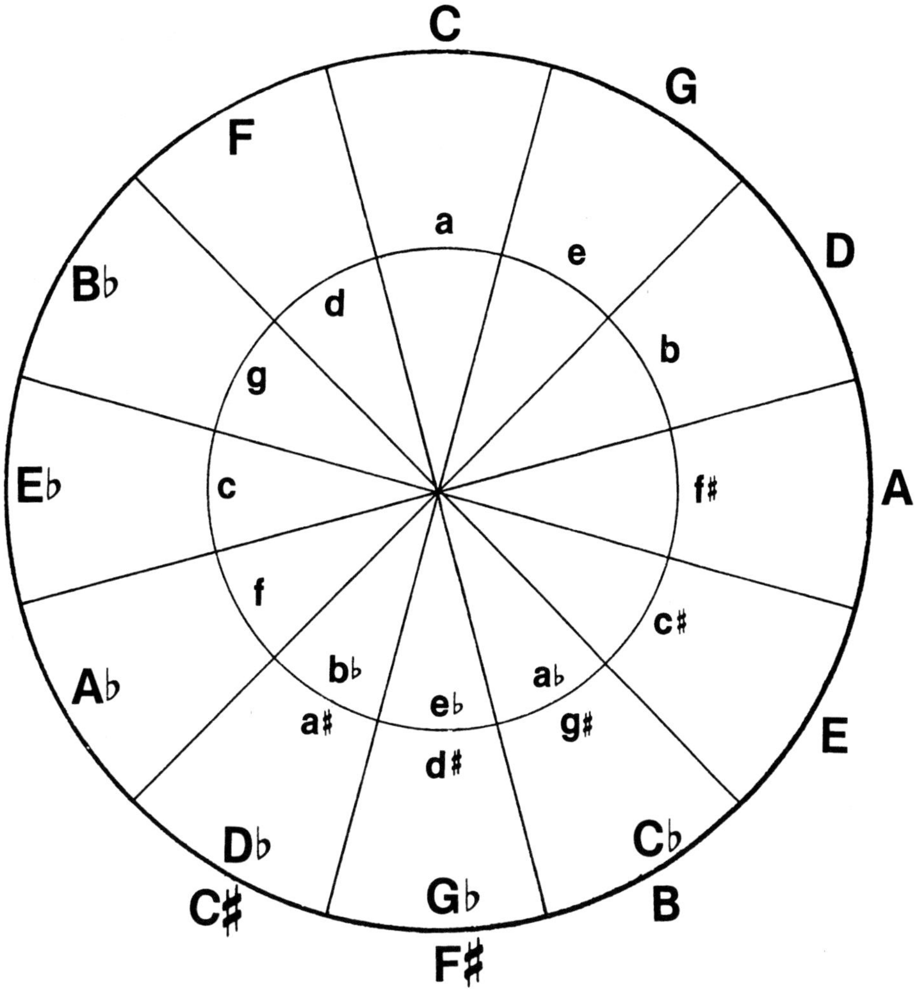

There are three types of minor scales:

(1) The *natural* or *pure* minor scale uses the notes indicated by the key signature with no alterations.

A B C D E F G A

(2) The *harmonic* minor scale has the seventh note of the scale raised one half-step.

A B C D E F G# A

(3) The *melodic* minor scale has the sixth and the seventh notes of the scale raised one half-step when ascending. (Notice that it is actually a major scale with a lowered third note.)

A B C D E F# G# A

The descending melodic minor scale is the same as the natural minor.

A G F E D C B A

ENHARMONIC SCALES

The final three sharp scales and the final three flat scales overlap. A♯/B♭, D♯/E♭, G♯/A♭ are called enharmonic scales. The keys on the keyboard, the sounds, and the fingering are the same, but the written appearance is different.

A♯/B♭ Minor Scales

A♯ B♭	B♯ C	C♯ D♭	D♯ E♭	E♯ F	F♯ G♭	G♯ A♭	A♯ B♭

D♯/E♭ Minor Scales

D♯ E♭	E♯ F	F♯ G♭	G♯ A♭	A♯ B♭	B C♭	C♯ D♭	D♯ E♭

G♯/A♭ Minor Scales

G♯ A♭	A♯ B♭	B C♭	C♯ D♭	D♯ E♭	E F♭	F♯ G♭	G♯ A♭

LEARNING TO PLAY MINOR SCALES

THINGS TO DO ON PAGES 23 THROUGH 28:

I. LEARN THOROUGHLY ALL MINOR SCALES, *HANDS SEPARATELY*, ONE OCTAVE.

Be sure to keep the pulse steady and not to proceed to quicker note values until slower ones are securely played. The metronome may be used.

A. **Learn all minor scales that are fingered like their parallel majors, L.H. first, then R.H.**

1. Practice the major scale in half notes, then the parallel minor in half notes.
2. Practice the major scale in quarter notes, then the parallel minor in quarters.
3. Practice the major scale in eighth notes, then the parallel minor in eighths.

B. **Learn the remaining minor scales in groups, practicing one entire fingering group at a time.**

1. Practice them in half notes, quarter notes, and eighth notes.

II. INCREASE THE NUMBER OF OCTAVES, *HANDS SEPARATELY*.

A. **Practice all scales in one fingering group two octaves in half notes.**
B. **Practice them one octave in quarter notes.**
C. **Practice them two octaves in eighth notes.**
D. **Practice them three octaves in triplet eighth notes.**
E. **Practice them four octaves in sixteenth notes.**

III. **VARY THE ARTICULATION, DYNAMICS, AND DIRECTION AS WAS DONE WITH THE MAJOR SCALES ON PAGE 10.**

MINOR SCALES — LEFT HAND

These scales are "free." Learn no new fingering.

THESE NINE MINOR SCALES ARE FINGERED EXACTLY LIKE THEIR PARALLEL MAJORS.

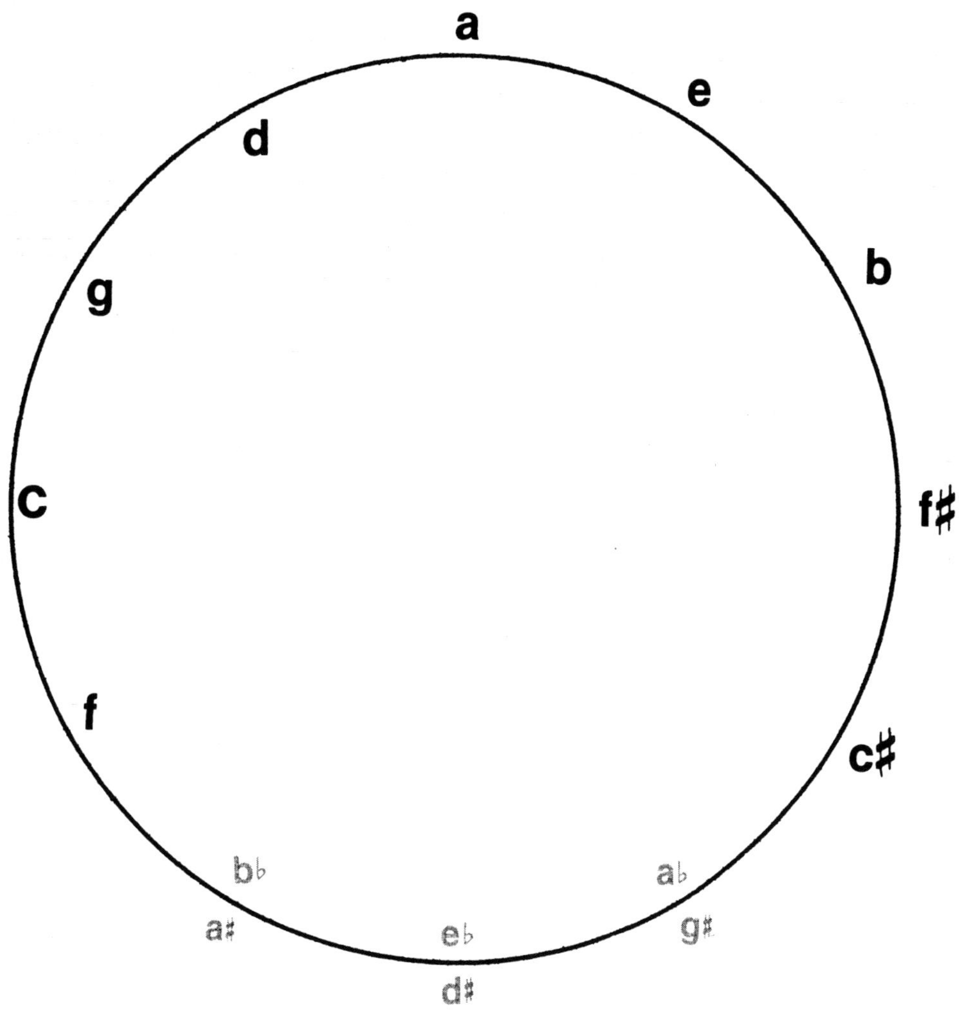

> ***REMEMBER:***
> Finger exactly like the parallel major

MINOR SCALES — LEFT HAND

NATURAL MINOR AND DESCENDING MELODIC:
THE FOURTH FINGER PLAYS F♯/G♭. (RULE OF 3 BLACK KEYS)

HARMONIC MINOR AND ASCENDING MELODIC:
FINGER EXACTLY LIKE A♭ MAJOR. (FOURTH FINGER PLAYS D♭ [C♯])

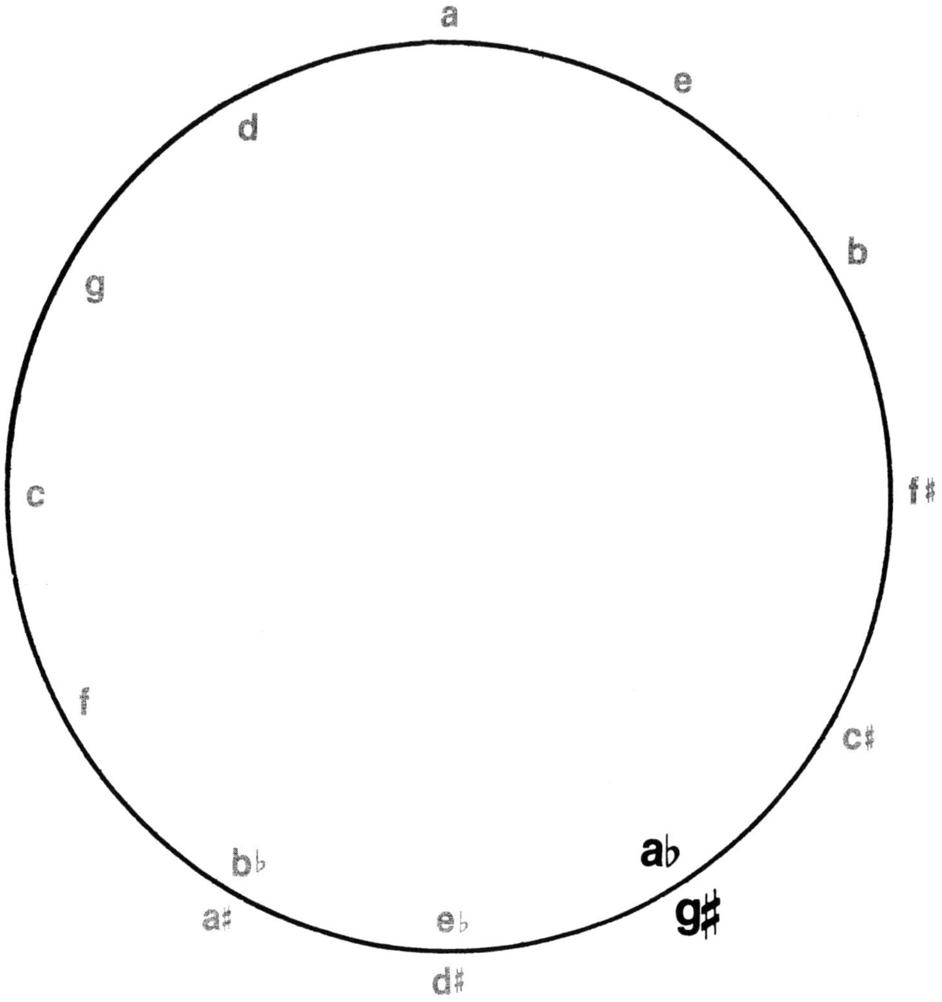

REMEMBER:

Natural and Descending Melodic

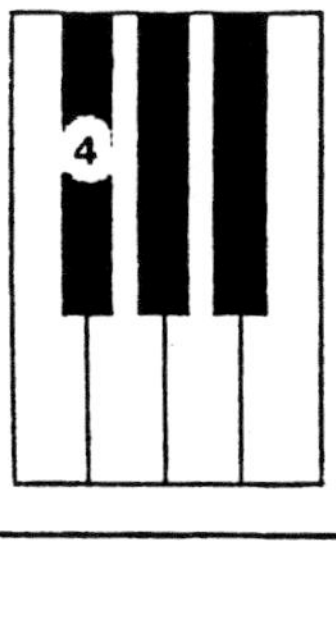

Harmonic and Ascending Melodic

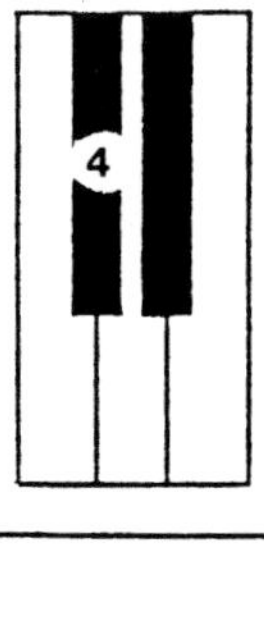

MINOR SCALES — LEFT HAND

These four scales use the Rule of 3 Black Keys.

RULE OF 3 BLACK KEYS:
THE FOURTH FINGER OF THE LEFT HAND PLAYS THE LOWEST KEY OF THE THREE BLACK KEY GROUP.

To discover the beginning finger, place the fourth finger on G♭/F♯and descend to the tonic. (Example: E♭ /D♯ Minor – play 4 on G♭/F♯, cross 1 under on F/E♯, 2 on E♭/D♯. 2 is the beginning finger.)

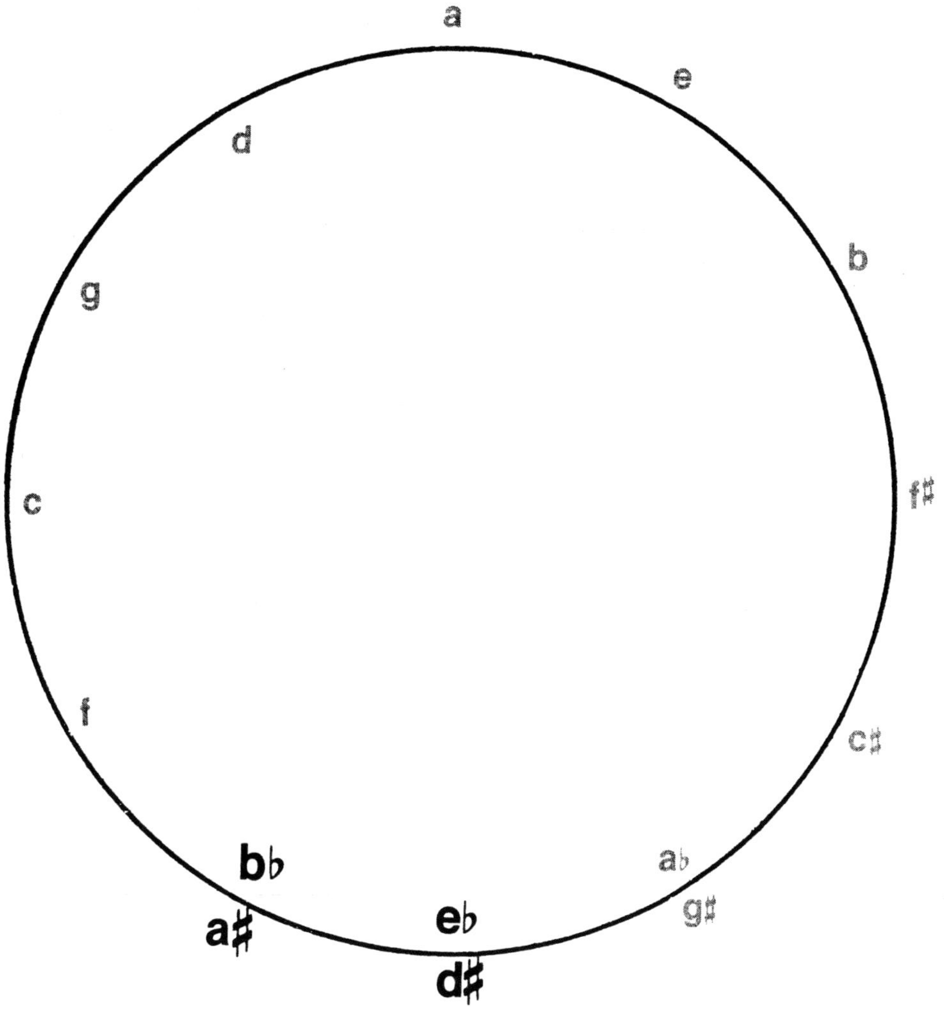

REMEMBER:

Rule of 3 Black Keys

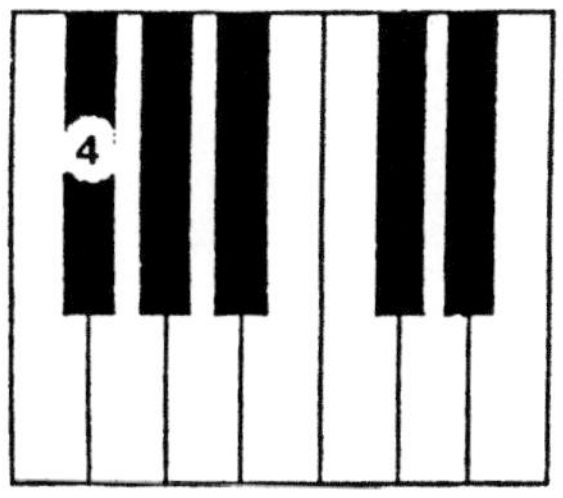

MINOR SCALES — RIGHT HAND

These scales are "free." Learn no new fingering.

THESE THIRTEEN MINOR SCALES ARE FINGERED EXACTLY LIKE THEIR PARALLEL MAJORS.

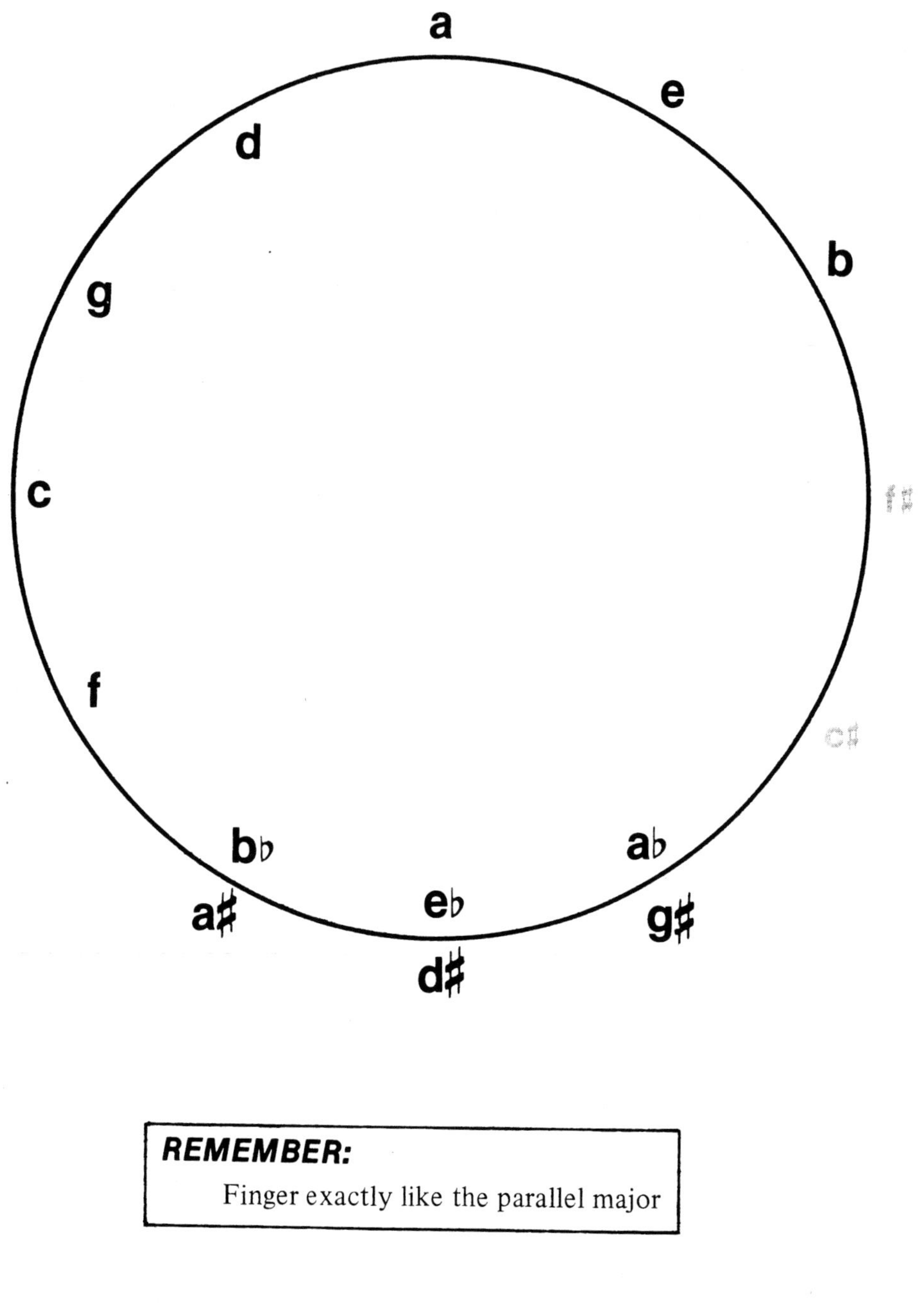

> ***REMEMBER:***
> Finger exactly like the parallel major

MINOR SCALES — RIGHT HAND

NATURAL MINOR, HARMONIC MINOR, AND DESCENDING MELODIC MINOR:
THE FOURTH FINGER PLAYS THE SECOND NOTE OF THE SCALE. (NOTICE THAT THE DESCENDING MELODIC BEGINS WITH THE THIRD FINGER ON THE HIGHEST NOTE.)

To discover the beginning finger, place the fourth finger on the second key of the scale and descend to the tonic. (Example: F♯ Minor – play 4 on G♯, 3 on F♯. 3 is the beginning finger.)

ASCENDING MELODIC MINOR:
THE FOURTH FINGER PLAYS THE SIXTH NOTE OF THE SCALE. (NOTICE THAT THE RULE OF 3 BLACK KEYS APPLIES TO C♯.)

To discover the beginning finger, place the fourth finger on the sixth key of the scale and descend to the tonic. (Example: F♯Minor – play 4 on D♯, 3 on C♯, 2 on B, 1 on A, cross 3 over on G♯, 2 on F♯. 2 is the beginning finger.)

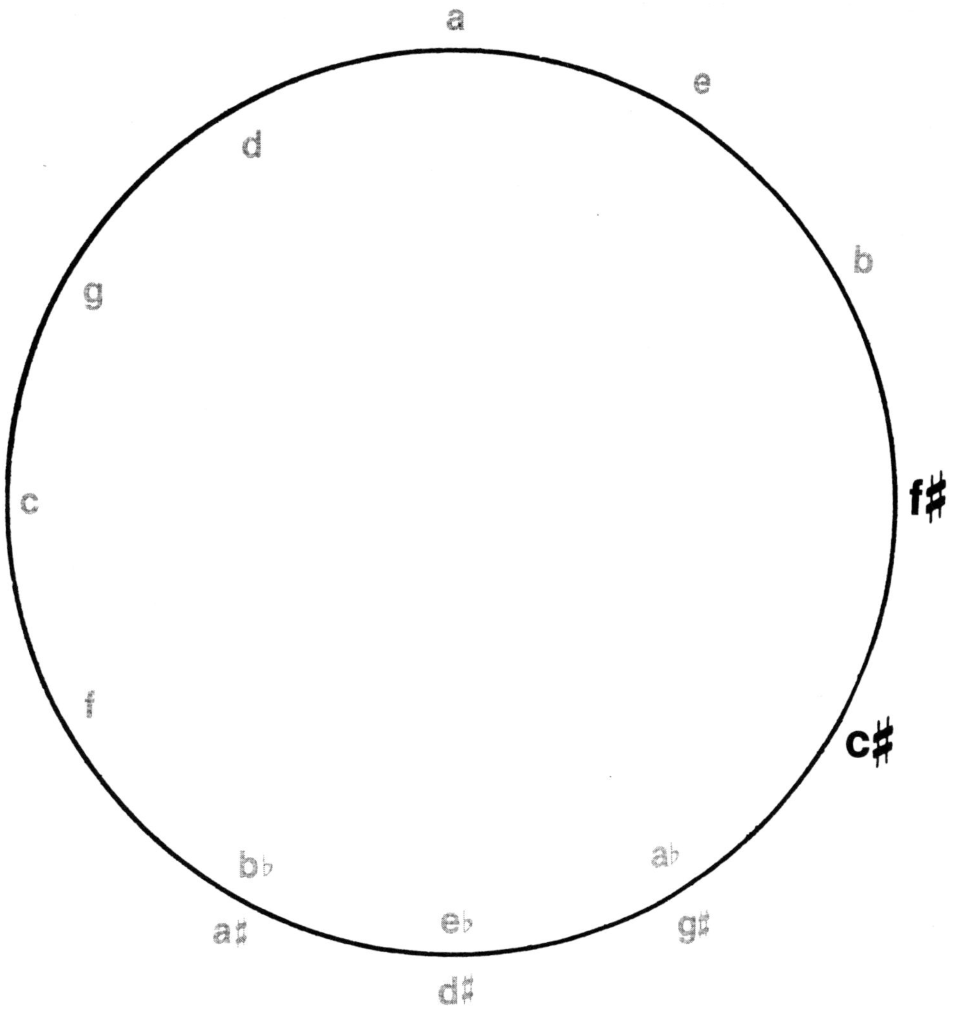

REMEMBER:
Natural, harmonic, and descending melodic: 4th on 2nd note.
Ascending melodic: 4th on 6th note.

CIRCLE OF 5THS
MINOR SCALE FINGERING — SUMMARY

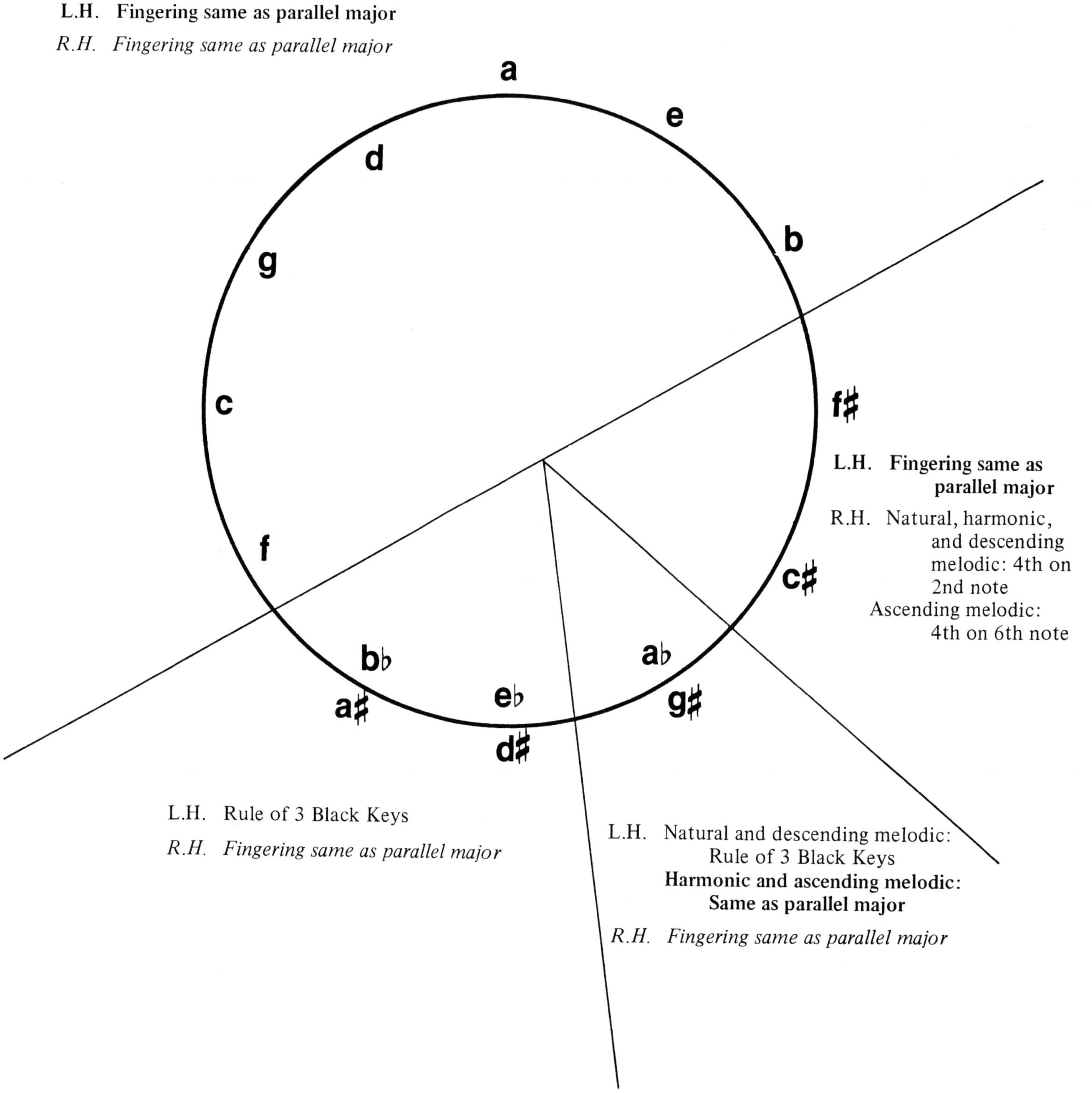

LEARNING TO PLAY MINOR SCALES

THINGS TO DO ON PAGES 30 THROUGH 32:

I. LEARN ALL THE MINOR SCALES, HANDS TOGETHER, ONE OCTAVE. LEARN ALL SCALES IN ONE FINGERING GROUP TOGETHER. PRACTICE THEM IN HALF NOTES, QUARTER NOTES, AND EIGHTH NOTES.

The pulse must always be steady. Learn the scales thoroughly one octave in half notes before proceeding to quicker note values and more octaves.

A. Group 1 contains A, E, D, G, and C. Play the parallel major scale before playing each minor scale.
B. Group 2 contains F and B. Play the parallel major scale before playing each minor scale.
C. Group 3 contains E♭/D♯and B♭/A♯.
D. Group 4 contains A♭ /G♯ , F♯ , and C♯. Each of these scales should be learned singly.

II. INCREASE THE NUMBER OF OCTAVES.
A. Practice all scales in one group two octaves in half notes.
B. Practice them one octave in quarter notes.
C. Practice them two octaves in eighth notes.
D. Practice them three octaves in triplet eighth notes.
D. Practice them four octaves in sixteenth notes.

III. VARY THE DIRECTION, THE INTERVALS BETWEEN THE HANDS, THE ARTICULATION, THE DYNAMICS, AND THE RHYTHM AS WAS DONE WITH THE MAJOR SCALES ON PAGE 17.

MINOR SCALES
HANDS TOGETHER — PARALLEL MOTION

When playing scales, hands together, it is helpful to notice that:

(1) Scales always use alternating groups of three and four fingers.
(1 2 3) (1 2 3 4) or (1 2 3 4) (1 2 3)

(2) In most scales certain same fingers will always play together.

A, E, B, D, G, C, and F minor scales use the same fingering as their parallel major scales. There is no need to relearn these fingerings. Just change the key signature to play these scales.

Notice in the following group of scales:

(1) Third fingers always play together.

(2) Fourth fingers surround the tonic. (L.H. 4 is above the tonic. R.H. 4 is below the tonic.)

A

	1	2	3	1	2	3	4	5(1)
Natural	A	B	C	D	E	F	G	A
Harmonic	A	B	C	D	E	F	G♯	A
Ascending	A	B	C	D	E	F♯	G♯	A
Melodic	5(1)	4	3	2	1	3	2	1

E

	1	2	3	1	2	3	4	5(1)
Natural	E	F♯	G	A	B	C	D	E
Harmonic	E	F♯	G	A	B	C	D♯	E
Ascending	E	F♯	G	A	B	C♯	D♯	E
Melodic	5(1)	4	3	2	1	3	2	1

D

	1	2	3	1	2	3	4	5(1)
Natural	D	E	F	G	A	B♭	C	D
Harmonic	D	E	F	G	A	B♭	C♯	D
Ascending	D	E	F	G	A	B♮	C♯	D
Melodic	5(1)	4	3	2	1	3	2	1

G

	1	2	3	1	2	3	4	5(1)
Natural	G	A	B♭	C	D	E♭	F	G
Harmonic	G	A	B♭	C	D	E♭	F♯	G
Ascending	G	A	B♭	C	D	E♮	F♯	G
Melodic	5(1)	4	3	2	1	3	2	1

C

	1	2	3	1	2	3	4	5(1)
Natural	C	D	E♭	F	G	A♭	B♭	C
Harmonic	C	D	E♭	F	G	A♭	B♮	C
Ascending	C	D	E♭	F	G	A♮	B♮	C
Melodic	5(1)	4	3	2	1	3	2	1

Notice in the following group of scales:
(1) Thumbs always play together.

		1	2	3	4	1	2	3	4(1)
F	Natural	F	G	A♭	B♭	C	D♭	E♭	F
	Harmonic	F	G	A♭	B♭	C	D♭	E♮	F
	Ascending	F	G	A♭	B♭	C	D♮	E♮	F
	Melodic	5(1)	4	3	2	1	3	2	1

		1	2	3	1	2	3	4	5(1)
B	Natural	B	C♯	D	E	F♯	G	A	B
	Harmonic	B	C♯	D	E	F♯	G	A♯	B
	Ascending	B	C♯	D	E	F♯	G♯	A♯	B
	Melodic	4(1)	3	2	1	4	3	2	1

Notice in this group of scales:
(1) Thumbs always play together.

		3	1	2	3	4	1	2	3
E♭	Natural	E♭	F	G♭	A♭	B♭	C♭	D♭	E♭
	Harmonic	E♭	F	G♭	A♭	B♭	C♭	D♮	E♭
	Ascending Melodic	E♭	F	G♭	A♭	B♭	C♮	D♮	E♭
D♯	Natural	D♯	E♯	F♯	G♯	A♯	B	C♯	D♯
	Harmonic	D♯	E♯	F♯	G♯	A♯	B	C♯♯	D♯
	Ascending	D♯	E♯	F♯	G♯	A♯	B♯	C♯♯	D♯
	Melodic	2	1	4	3	2	1	3	2

		4	1	2	3	1	2	3	4
B♭	Natural	B♭	C	D♭	E♭	F	G♭	A♭	B♭
	Harmonic	B♭	C	D♭	E♭	F	G♭	A♮	B♭
	Ascending Melodic	B♭	C	D♭	E♭	F	G♮	A♮	B♭
A♯	Natural	A♯	B♯	C♯	D♯	E♯	F♯	G♯	A♯
	Harmonic	A♯	B♯	C♯	D♯	E♯	F♯	G♯♯	A♯
	Ascending	A♯	B♯	C♯	D♯	E♯	F♯♯	G♯♯	A♯
	Melodic	2	1	3	2	1	4	3	2

Notice in this scale:

(1) Third fingers play together on C♯.

(2) Thiru and fourth fingers play together on the remaining black keys.

F♯		3	4	1	2	3	1	2	3
	Natural	F♯	G♯	A	B	C♯	D	E	F♯
	Harmonic	F♯	G♯	A	B	C♯	D	E♯	F♯
		4	3	2	1	3	2	1	4

Notice in this scale:

(1) Third fingers always play together.

F♯		2	3	1	2	3	4	1	2
	Ascending Melodic	F♯	G♯	A	B	C♯	D♯	E♯	F♯
		4	3	2	1	3	2	1	4

Notice in this scale:

(1) Third fingers always play together.

C♯		3	4	1	2	3	1	2	3
	Natural	C♯	D♯	E	F♯	G♯	A	B	C♯
	Harmonic	C♯	D♯	E	F♯	G♯	A	B♯	C♯
		3	2	1	4	3	2	1	3

Notice in this scale:

(1) Thumbs always play together.

C♯		2	3	1	2	3	4	1	2
	Ascending Melodic	C♯	D♯	E	F♯	G♯	A♯	B♯	C♯
		3	2	1	4	3	2	1	3

Notice in this scale:

(1) Thumbs play together.

		3	4	1	2	3	1	2	3
G♯	Natural	G♯	A♯	B	C♯	D♯	E	F♯	G♯
A♭	Natural	A♭	B♭	C♭	D♭	E♭	F♭	G♭	A♭
		3	2	1	3	2	1	4	3

Notice in this scale:

(1) Third fingers always play together.

		3	4	1	2	3	1	2	3
G♯	Harmonic	G♯	A♯	B	C♯	D♯	E	F♯♯	G♯
	Ascending Melodic	G♯	A♯	B	C♯	D♯	E♯	F♯♯	G♯
A♭	Harmonic	A♭	B♭	C♭	D♭	E♭	F♭	G♮	A♭
	Ascending Melodic	A♭	B♭	C♭	D♭	E♭	F♮	G♮	A♭
		3	2	1	4	3	2	1	3